CENTURIES

Also by Joel Brouwer

Exactly What Happened

CENTURIES
Prose poems

Joel Brouwer

Four Way Books
New York City

**Distributed by
University Press
of New England
Hanover and London**

Editorial Office
Four Way Books
PO Box 535, Village Station
New York, NY 10014
www.fourwaybooks.com

Library of Congress
Catalog Card Number: 2002110847

ISBN: 1-884800-39-4

Book Design: Brunel
Cover Art: elin o'Hara slavick

This book is manufactured in the United States of America and
printed on acid-free paper.

Four Way Books is a division of Friends of Writers, Inc.,
a Vermont-based not-for-profit organization. We are grateful
for the assistance we receive from individual donors and
private foundations.

Distributed by University Press of New England,
One Court Street, Lebanon, NH 03766.

CONTENTS

for elin o'Hara slavick
comrade!

It takes just one awful second, I often think, and an entire epoch passes.

—W. G. Sebald, *The Rings of Saturn*
(translated by Michael Hulse)

5000

Telegram: my pal John the Baptist beheaded by smack. At the Central Park rowboat rental shack I pick a sky-blue with splintered oars and limp across the lake. I beg heaven to bring John back. It answers in hailstones. A crowd of pigeons gathers on the shore. I preach that junkies are already dead; stopped hearts are mere formality. I invent malignitudes: doomed are those who ask for it, etc. One bird coos, *Enough yakking, Mac. We're hungry.* I pinch crumbs from my pocket. They're just specks! Meager as words! But they somehow suffice: the faithful eat and are satisfied.

Debut

People keep saying to see the new opera. The main character, this aspiring artist, a man of modest talent who's destroyed by fate, reminds them, eerily, of you. You're curious, of course. You go by the theater just to look at the posters, but as you're walking through the alley the stage door flies open and the director is there, frantic, screaming, *You're on in ten minutes, where have you been,* and you realize you're naked under your coat, you don't remember a single line, and you'll have to go on like that, you'll have to go on and sing.

Bridge

He's terrified of sharks, so when the storm nails them to the bridge back from the Keys, he snaps: the bridge will buckle, the car will drop like a cartoon anvil to the Gulf's sandy floor, a hammerhead will tear them open like pillows of blood. *Plus barracuda,* she reminds him. Thanks. She says the bridge can take it, the bridge will hold, but then why's it swaying like a drunken tugboat? *That's exactly why it won't break. It gives a little.* It gives too goddamn much. She stops the car. Sharks circle. Here they are: home again so soon.

Bicycle

Papa promised: *If you behave during this war, help Mama haul water and stay away from tanks, you'll have a present.* I was good. I kept my hair and blisters in a jar and knit them into mittens for our neighbors. I stewed dud grenades so well my brother guessed venison. I grew huge rifles in our garden. I kicked gold from dead mouths to buy Mama oranges from the market. I bled freely, grinning like a saint. And after the war Papa carried home a blue bicycle with no wheels. Perfect! I had given my legs to the General.

Explanations

You mistook sex for architecture and climbed a ladder inside her to examine a cornice. You found a glass box packed with feathers and ashes. It fell from your fingers and shattered. You fell after it. You cracked your back. You made her mad. She turned into water and that's why the tanker went down with all hands. The feathers flew to Ecuador and that's why the Pope got shot. You kept the ashes, and that's why this morning the trees are full of arsonists and you'll wake up with a red-handled hatchet perched in your fist like a bird.

Childhood

Surrounded by ragweed and burdock. The silo, crumbling then, invisible now. A nimbus of squirrel skulls glowing yellow in the dirt. My memory as empty. Did I climb to the barn's lightning rod, or just threaten? We weren't farmers. In summer, the dead man's fields, ours via probate caprice, sprouted gladiolus, blueberries, rhubarb. We watched bewildered, filled vases and bowls, but most of it rotted where it stood. The daffodils still come up without me to cut, rubber-band, and sell them by the roadside. Four cars a day came by. Here's the rusty coffee can I dreamed full of dimes.

Diagnosis

The doctor says, *Think of it this way. Your insides are like the jungle at night: warm, noisy, rank with mango, and but for some holes drilled through the sky by stars, wholly dark. A river floats through you on its back, shivering with silver piranhas. Banyan roots claw its face with thirsty fingers and draw black water up to the leafy canopy, where the last honeysuckle vireo on earth has sunk her beak into the single living pygmy anaconda, which in turn has the bird half wrapped in its flexing grip. Only one will live. It's too soon to say.*

Marked

God marked Cain so we would know to curse him, but who pushed the teapot from the pantry shelf and cut Francine's cheek? And why? The scar glows white when she's cold: rice grain in a dish of milk. In Egypt, death passed doors daubed with lamb's blood but in Poland stopped at those chalked with a star. The pencil salesman's son hides upstairs, painting encyclopedia pages white. His father's shadow pours into the room like ink into water. *You have to make a mark upon the world!* Rain beats a clear tattoo on the roof. *Yes, Sir. Hold still.*

Father

Confronted with eye charts he'd fake a squint, then recite Lear letter by letter: *L-E-S-T I-T S-E-E M-O-R-E, P-R-E-V-E-N-T I-T. O-U-T, F-O-U-L J-E-L-L-Y!* The doctor shook his head, fidgeted with a clipboard. Night fell like a wheelchair dropped from a roof. Father said, *Beautiful day.* At home I propped him up in bed, whence he issued decrees: *Distinguished thing my ass! More light! We owe Asklepios a pot roast!* One night I caught him in the living room, winding back the hands of the moonlit clock and crying. *Pray undo this button,* he whispered. Then: *No, stay away. It's contagious.*

Aesthetics

Your brother has leukemia? Carve ivory. The elections were rigged? Write a villanelle. A girl shivers in streetlight, takes off her mittens, pulls a silver yo-yo from her pocket. Dogs bark behind a fence. Use oil on wood. Concentrate on pacing when choreographing your divorce; you will have to move through it forever. Two men in green fatigues tie a woman flat to a metal table. One has a rubber hose, the other a pliers. A third man arrives with sandwiches and a thermos. A body has soft and hard parts, like a piano. Music comes from where they meet.

Serena

One autumn, years after you fucked me to shreds and vanished, I visited Anna at her studio upstate. We walked the stubbled fields, drank wine beneath a yellow willow, and after dinner she showed me some canvases. One was of you: stretched nude in a green chair, your fingers even longer, skin even deeper burnt umber than I remembered. Anna was amazed. *I didn't know her. She modeled at the colony last summer.* Today, years since I saw Anna, someone behind me on the snowy sidewalk calls *Serena!* Lost one, what's become of me? I thought of the painting first.

Vodka

The Stoli bottle's frost melts to brilliance where I press my
fingers. Evidence. Proof I'm here, drunk in your lamplit kitchen,
breathing up your rented air, no intention of leaving. Our lust
squats blunt as a brick on the table between us. We're low on
vocabulary. We're *vodkaquiet. Vodkadeliquescent.* Vodka doesn't
like theatrics: it walks into your midnight bedroom already
naked, slips in beside you, takes your shoulders in its icy hands
and shoves. Is that a burglar at the window? *No, he lives with
me, actually.* Well, let him in for Christ's sake, let's actually get this
over with.

N

So much that's not nice: *napalm, nettles, nemesis, noose*. Not to mention the basic *no*. Even the dictionary's blissful path from *neck* to *nectar*—a trembling fingertip gliding over her nipple, down around her navel—is choked by morbid vines from the intervening *necro-* root: *-mania, -phagia, -philia*. A few pages later, too fractious to define, six single-spaced columns of *non-*'s. N's headquarters: Nuremberg. Motto: *Non possumus*. Hometown heroes: Nero, Nixon, and poisonous Nessus. In algebra it nastily conceals the answer. *Solve for* n, says Mrs. Needle, twitching her ruler across your knuckles. *And remember, ninnies:* n *can be anything*.

for James Wagner

Proposal

Now, while radios crackle my latest victims' names and the colors
their blood made on the sidewalk—cabernet, eggplant, mud—
say yes. In the middle of the list. Would you be more comfortable
strolling out behind the slaughterhouse? Shall we take another
stumble through the burn ward? Here's a note from my parole
board and a snapshot of my Dumpster. Here's a list of my
prescriptions in order of importance. Now while tornadoes screw
the city, now half-drowned in sobs, now as I tear our last dollar
to confetti. Toss off your drink and dress. Look at me. Say yes.

Idea

Half-complete before you realized your hands were moving. If only you'd finished it that way! But now you hold it to the light, narrow your eyes, the mind's oily brass pistons begin to fire . . . a Reichstag visible only through special goggles. Grab your jacket, you're off to the patent office again. The boy with the piccolo stumbles in as you rush out; you tip your hat and nod. While you draft blueprints all afternoon, he'll wobble around your yard in his uniform of whiskey, playing aimlessly, leading his cheering roach and rat disciples up and down the half-finished spaceship's steps.

after Fellini

Master

Parents offered their finest sons as pupils; rejects were dropped down wells. One boy walked as if a dove were roosting on his head. At this the Master smiled. He taught the child to saw bonbons in half with a tiny, jeweled knife, discern superior doilies from inferior, wave when armies marched by. He inspected his body: flawless as milk, save the pimply, swollen mouth. *My final gift*, the Master droned, kissing the angry blot, which then issued buckets of honey. Now the pupil was impeccable. So was sent to the cellar, where he lives on crickets with the others.

Meadow

A man crosses a meadow choked with weeds, broken concrete, rusted machinery, pausing every few steps to throw a stone. What danger these scouts are meant to flush from hiding you don't know. The air is hot and sweet, like rotten melon or a lit fuse. The man moves slowly, like a frightened submarine. He sings a folk song: *My children eat and drink. Webbed fingers help them swim. We are put on earth a short time.* That night you approach his campfire. He offers a potato. You have nothing to trade but a story: *A man crosses a meadow . . .*

after Tarkovsky

Michigan

Smoke a pack of Kools in the dunes. Then he'll push your hand down his swimsuit. Hold the damp cold there. Smell alewives. Then he'll do you, and that's it. Back to the campground. No talking. Coppertone, hamburgers, Frisbee. Suggest a walk on the pier to see if the fish are biting, though you couldn't care less. *Too small, son. We're throwing them back.* Good soldier-talk to remember for later, when someone's older brother wants payback for the rum and the storm's chasing boats to harbor like a dog after rabbits. *Fish biting, kid?* Too small. They're throwing them back.

Recluse

He isn't lonely. Each part of him stays up late, playing bridge, eating pretzels. Toes do cigarette tricks, the tongue recites Dickinson. Fingers thread a faded print of *Grand Hotel* through the rickety projector, dim the lights, and the eyes watch Garbo flicker like a moth in a jar. When everything else has drifted to sleep, the recluse and his penis sip brandy and reminisce. *Ah, Elba,* sighs the penis. Night gathers on the porch with microphones and cameras. The recluse turns the lock, tugs absently at his bandages. *Yes, it seems like yesterday. But even today seems like yesterday.*

Clearing

You breathe easier in the clearing, as if a stone were lifted from your chest or the voltage lowered. Before that, everything's awkward, you never know what's next: suicides, firefights, screaming families. In the truck someone has to pull the rice sack over the prisoner's head, tie his hands. You can't help touching the skin. The trail through the jungle is muddy, and when you're leading him you sometimes slip, catch yourself on his shoulder, feel him shiver. It's embarrassing. In the clearing things are simple. The moon glints in a tilted bottle. You have a shovel or a gun.

Wedding

My sisters Martha and Mary taught me to dance like a ladder while my mother sang a song called *Sell Me Money*. My mother will come back in the end. Martha lacquered her face with strawberry jam; Mary unfolded towels. When I regained self-consciousness they were pushing me down the corridor like a stalled car and I'd gone wrong in my pants. I wanted to nail the apples back onto the tree but couldn't find a hammer. I chopped out my mouth but nights I still hear it, down at the dump, telling dirty stories to the eggshells. My mother.

Disease

One day—you're ice skating, or baking bread—it assaults the body's capital, raises flags of fatigue and bruise. And the mind, abstracted as Louis in Versailles, understands it has an enemy, but cannot imagine its face. Drop of blood on a blanket. Drop of blood in ginger ale. Drop of blood on television. Pharmaceutical battalions in pink and yellow helmets float downward to darkness above your marshes. The intern cleans her knife in a weedy stream. You give and rescind stool samples, read mystery novels backwards in your bunker. Cover up those daffodils, Corporal—they'll give your position away.

Party

While everyone else admires the host's gigantic children, who move naked through the crowd with trays of champagne and braised finch wings, the host himself keeps steering you toward the garage and a cigar box full of nails. *Oh, they're delicious,* he says, pretending to eat a handful as he locks the door behind him. The garage smells of turpentine and dirty magazines. The freezer hums with meat. You pour yourself an insecticide martini, scratch idly at your wart, and chit-chat with a cricket. *Well, I'd better get home—my wife will be worried.* Even the mice know you're lying.

Zokar

We fled a dull party via the fire escape, ran six rainy blocks down Amsterdam to her father's apartment. Her throat glowed in streetlight like a wet Vermeer. The place was stuffed with silk pillows and sandalwood. Spotlit crystal dolphins splashed rainbows on the wall. *Um, what's your father's deal?* (We're naked now.) *He channels Zokar, a citizen of Atlantis. Troubled people come, Dad summons Zokar, and Zokar gives them succor.* We ran the bath, giggling like mermaids. I shouted, *I am possessed by barracuda!* and she shushed me with salty kisses as our doomed continent sank beneath the waves.

Lana Turner

You'll claim you found the POWs after careful recon, crawled in at dawn to free them. In fact, you'd gone behind a bush to imagine Lana Turner and there they were: fingers woven through chainlink, faces ash, watching you clutch at yourself. You zipped up, sawed awkwardly at the fence; they said, *Better let us do that.* You offered maps; they spilled silently into the woods. Dogs barked. A hole popped open wetly on your leg. In Hollywood, Lana Turner tossed in her sleep and loosed a small, soft fart, which drifted up over her bed like an observation balloon.

Forgiveness

Our ship sank near Italy. We took turns at raft and survivor: days I rode her, nights she rode me. Sharks bladed ocean beneath us. I heard mermaids singing. She said *mirage* but that's only in deserts. We stumbled ashore and followed the song to a cathedral, the falsetto C's bright as needles in moonlight. We pressed together in the tiny booth, confessed at length and in unison, demonstrating those sins for which there are no words. When we emerged, exhausted with forgiveness, the castrati surrounded us: giants, matted with hair, squeaking in fury and shaking their huge, futile fists.

after Antonioni

Demonstration

At dawn we painted slogans on bedsheets. It was still dark: we couldn't see what we were saying. At the demonstration we smoked joints behind a Dumpster like it was a party. A man was dancing with a flag, a woman was screaming at a flag, the flags were introduced, hit it off, walked off together holding hands. The man and woman shrugged and caught a cab. Cops floated through the crowd on horses, giving Latin lessons and collecting teeth. And later we slept in the sheets we'd waved at the cameras, our convictions flaking off in brittle red splinters.

Ambition

At the ceremony some hack starts eating my chicken. When I reach for wine he snaps at my wrist with a giant scissors. Excuse me, are you leaking money? My foot's stuck in a puddle of it. The committee repeats last year's mistake, announcing I've won but pronouncing my name so badly someone else bounds down to the stage. I drive home thinking *hot shower* but this no-talent bastard's moved into my house. Through the window I see him waltzing with Alfred Nobel. Then they're kissing. The pencil in my pocket begins to tremble—villanelle? sestina?—then blurts *remember eggs*.

Heaven

The night the poet was rejected he took his goat to the ocean and threw beached, wormy fish back into the surf. His goat, meanwhile, rooted through dunes of garbage left by that day's sunbathers. The poet said, *Just as these fish, restored to their element, tumble among the waves in vain parody of swimming, so I, though I walk the earth like men, am no man. I am a puppet, jerked through my days by the strings of the wind.* The moon turned its back. Gulls sobbed overhead. The goat said, *I'm in ice-cream sandwich wrapper heaven over here.*

Detroit

Snow plunges down the night, scatters in gritty bursts above the vacant lots like salt into the fields of Carthage. I'm sixteen stories above, watching the bedlam rush up and down the window like a biology-class film of blood cells lunging at the gates of the heart and falling back repulsed, like your breath through the telephone rising with *Florida* and falling with *Never*. Through the cracks in the sidewalk below, spidery arms of chickweed clutch at women torn from magazines, spin them in a frozen cotillion. If every streetlight on the block's shot out, where's that glow coming from?

Court-Martial

Your Honor, for the thousandth time. Pretty much everyone was on fire. Our boys wore red, the enemy wore red. It's easier that way. My rifle kept turning into puzzle pieces, sand, cherry pits . . . I was scared. Then this redhead, a real knockout, steps out of the flames with cups and a punchbowl. I noticed some limes floating around. Then I blew her guts out. Wouldn't anyone with sense? She smiled. Her teeth sparked like an experiment. Her eyes smoked. And yes we drank the punch that night. The CO hadn't told us yet! Sir, how could we have known?

Ideas

Arrive unannounced, radiator fuming, honk shave-and-a-haircut in the driveway. *Just passing through,* they grin, unloading their suitcases. Cousins, maybe, or forgotten college pals: they're somehow yours and you have to take them in. At dinner he details business schemes—drive-through psychology, pet vacations—for which he requires investors. She drinks a whole bottle of wine, licks her lips at your teenage son. Their baby purples with the shrill, halting cry of a stabbed bird. And when they've left the house silent again, its dusty rooms suddenly uncrossable deserts, you try everything—telegrams, ultimatums, ritual dance—anything to get them back.

Noah

Nights I gave lectures and slide shows on deck: "Leprosy," "Pol Pot," "The Trail of Tears." Attendance was mandatory, as were daily visits to the torture-implements exhibit in the hold. *THINK IT OVER* said the signs. I hung mirrors everywhere, fed carnivores hay, herbivores each other. After forty days they were stumbling the decks in terror, dazed with the grief of being. I ran us aground and distributed ballots. Almost everyone, thank God, voted to suicide, but a few half-wits refused, marched off across the damp summit clutching their wrinkled testicles and breasts, eyes narrowed against the bright, birdless air.

Tiramisù

Italian deli off the Vegas strip, prosciutti strung from the ceiling like Kewpie dolls. You bought tiramisù for my birthday cake. *Best west of Brooklyn,* said the fat brothers behind the counter. Remember? You poured Chianti into paper cups, struck a match as a candle. I made a wish. It came true. We swam the Desert Star Motel's tepid yellow pool, gorged the slots with nickels, made love across our room's rotten bed. Your neon skin glowed blue as an X ray's broken bone. I could almost see by you. *Tiramisù.* Do you know it means *lift me up?* You did.

Joyce

I bring "The Dead" to read in my cubicle but Nurse says, *No novels.* I protest: *It's a novella!* She rolls her eyes. I'm wondering where subjects go once an experiment's over. Did Pavlov's dogs get names and loving homes? Did Lorenz eat his geese? The buzzer buzzes. Now I press the blue lever twice and make twenty bucks, or the red ten times for a hit. My summer job. Thirty per visit, fifty if I skip the dope. Joyce said, *A man of genius makes no mistakes.* Is it really an experiment if you know what's going to happen?

Hors d'Oeuvres

Platters of rabbit ovaries and bottles filled with wasps on the backyard picnic table. Night pushes its tongue across your neck like a plow. Your date left with the host hours ago. *For ice.* His wife chops a sofa in half with a chainsaw while you hold her baby. When it vomits, she spits into a napkin, says, *It's only natural.* You drive to the ocean, swigging stingers, the baby tossing robotic as a lobster on her lap. Out at sea, ships sink in whispers to let the sailors sleep. Together you watch the horizon pinch their white lights out.

Divorce

Got your letter. And the crate of dead crows. Are you trying to tell me something? Thought you might want to know—I'm taking a class on how to be a man. This week we learned that if you want to be one you can't be celery, a hotel room, or the Big Dipper. I raised my hand: *How about a crow?* The professor said, *Good, good! How* about *a crow?* We're graded on participation. Yes, you can keep the clock. Will you please send my hands and feet? They're in the nightstand, where you used to keep your fingers.

Crematorium

Who's dead today? the boss bellowed, picking up a clipboard. The morning's list was one line long: the boss's own daughter, who'd drowned. *Go home, sir,* his assistant choked. *I'll handle it today.* The boss lit a cigar, puffed wildly. *Nonsense!* he cried, screwing the cap from a red metal can. He threw the cigar in an ashtray, sloshed kerosene over the little wooden coffin, his chest and head, the floor and walls. *Dead is dead, my friend!* The arthritic dog curled in the corner—who really had no business being there—yawned, scratched at a flea, and fell asleep.

Hero

You wake to a brass band beneath your window and a crowd singing songs about your youth. Your children file by at attention, turn smart corners at the bedpost. You return their salutes. The kitchen's full of dignitaries cooking your breakfast, hanging bunting, blowing up balloons. The seated ones rise when you enter. Their medals clink like spoons on glasses. Someone hands you a speech: *I'm no hero,* it begins. A group of schoolchildren bustles in. You assume yesterday's pose. They open sketchbooks, sharpen pencils. All except the deaf boy, who just stares at his hands. *Pay attention!* you shout.

History

In Boston, a tongue of red paint traces the city's history, from Massacre to Tea Party to Faneuil Hall. We didn't listen. We were busy composing our own republic: delivering fiery speeches of popcorn to mobs of pigeons in the Commons, pledging allegiance in the green glow of the Aquarium's piranha tank. In the North End some traitor shouted, *Not in front of Paul Revere's house, youse! You'll raise him from the dead!* The red line led into our hotel, through our room, up the bedpost. Here history lifted her hips. Here the rebels put their desperate plan into motion.

Nova Scotia

Yesterday we dammed this creek with fist-sized stones, blocked its pulse to the ocean, but the storm's erased everything. Our affair's refrain: *We'll see, we'll see.* Standing in this valley with my hands full of gravel, I decide to expect henceforth only fire, tidal waves, and lions. To expect disasters and thus avoid disappointment. You stand on a boulder looking out over waves, your eyes avalanche, lips pure tornado, the world worlding in your hands. The moon looses its grip and water rushes forward drunk with ruin. Your little cousin hands me her birthday puppy, says, *I'm done with this.*

Ignorance

The authors you haven't read are cooking over campfires in your backyard. They've pitched tents and dug a well. You knew they'd eventually come to haunt you in their frock-coats and togas, wagging ink-stained fingers: *shame, shame.* But they don't seem irked: they sing as they peel potatoes, they've set up a volleyball net. You say, *I thought you'd be angry,* which cracks them up. *Hell no!* they roar. *Have some lunch!* Your mind floods with the morphine of relief. Someone ladles you a bowl of soup. You can see your face in there. You can see right through it.

Stray

Too weak to reach the doorbell, he crumples on your stoop in a puddle of fur and blood. When you step out for the newspaper he sobs like a foreign movie. The newspaper seems sulky too. Machine-gun fire from the hills? Well, the rebels might just be making dinner. And the mortars? Perhaps the army is having a square dance. Your neighbor agrees: it's a gorilla war and none of his business, he's strictly an orangutan mortician. You fetch a cracker, hold it high above the stray's pulpy head. He blows crimson bubbles through his nostrils. *Jump*, you say. *Jump*.

Mexico

We shit in a hole, got sand in our teeth, fought army ants in our sleep. Remember? I got so sick you had to cut my meat: pale cubes tough as dice. Then you got sick and I went swimming. That was wrong. But didn't I bring you a bucket of purple starfish, fetch fresh water from the *cenote*, kiss your griddle forehead? No. Those are lies. Sorry I told so many. You wanted to fuck and I kept pinching the yellow candle out. Sorry about the dark. Sorry I filled your head with eggs. Sorry I wasn't really sleepy.

Portage

Your mission: ferry all survivors downstream to Fort Babel. Colonel O'Thehorrorthehorror has promised strange, extravagant punishments for failure. The canoe's crowded. Your paddle laps weakly at the river. The survivors have their wounds in baskets, wrapped in stained paper, and take them out to nibble as they chat about blankets. Suddenly you hear the falls: a roar like the mobs at Nuremberg. You backpaddle, desperate for a portage, but the banks are vertical, stone, and infinite. The current's hand grasps your throat. You're going over again, like yesterday and the day before. The sky swings shut like an oven door.

Tumor

I lift your scalp like the lid on a pot of stew and firk the fucker
out. I've wondered for weeks which color it really was: the yellow
glow on the MRI, the encyclopedia diagram's green pecan, the
tiny blue crab from my dreams? You were no help. You slept and
slept. I quizzed interns over cafeteria trays: *Red like cherry Jell-O?*
Darker, like these beets? Sometimes I imagined it earthworm pink,
sometimes gray from all the brain it ate. Now here it is at last:
white as an empty ledger. Wake up, you bastard. I can't write
this alone.

Application

My current research concerns the mating habits of rust and the relation of same to the dreams of tropical birds. If awarded this grant, the funds would allow purchase of several rare aspic orchids indispensable to my work. Within weeks, nonexistent diseases will appear, wreak havoc, be cured, and pass into history. Most species of fish are named, gentlemen; many individual fish are not. A handwritten list of Europe's murder victims remains the final goal. With your support I can right these wrongs, and unforeseeable others. All that stands between us and success is a stack of airline tickets. Respectfully,

Amaryllis

To say, *Yes, I lied, but consider my position,* send three spiders in a
matchbox. Rubies and juniper are apologies. Sign your name
with blue ink if you want another chance, green for ambivalence,
red if you've torn your mouth from its hinges. A bird's nest warns
that desire obeys only itself. Twine says shame. You love her, but
love yourself more? Wrap a magnet in newspaper. Abalone means
We must resign ourselves to fate; paintbrushes *There is much I cannot
understand.* Cotton is astonishment. And if you know you must
speak, but not how or where to begin? Amaryllis.

after Fassbinder

Teacher

He stumbled in drunk, strumming a ukulele, suggested we all take off our shirts. It seemed fishy. But everyone says he's a genius, so OK, we thought, maybe it's a metaphor for something. Our first assignment: *Drink someone's blood. Not your own. Report via ghazal.* The next week he took us outside into a blizzard, pointed at the library and yelled, *What's that?* The wind babbled like a lunatic. *The library!* we shouted. He frowned, shook his head, asked again. Hours went by. Our tongues turned to ice. But we learned the lesson: walked away one by one, alone, cold.

Century

The art in the museum, exhausted and damp, demanded solitude. *We're tired of crying your tears! We hereby decree the purifying change and henceforth reject the trash! Now scram!* When curators offered to compromise by admitting only the blind, the art replied by suicide: each piece became a mirror. Beneath a bench we found a photograph of Eva Braun and Hitler locked in a deep wet kiss. She's nude, milk-blue against his black uniform. He has a riding crop in each hand. We shoved to see. Such a beautiful picture! It had to be: it was that or the mirrors.

ACKNOWLEDGMENTS

My thanks to the editors of the journals in which some of these poems first appeared:

AGNI	Century
	Detroit
	History
	Meadow
Arshile	Application
	Ideas
	Mexico
	Noah
	Portage
Artful Dodge	Clearing
	Crematorium
	Hero
The Blue Moon Review	Michigan
	N
The Cortland Review	Aesthetics
	Demonstration
	Joyce
DIAGRAM	Forgiveness
	Idea
Exquisite Corpse	Bicycle
	Court-Martial
	Divorce
	Explanations
	Hors d'Oeuvres
Hayden's Ferry Review	5000
	Proposal
Massachusetts Review	Father
Mudfish	Stray
	Tiramisù
Paris/Atlantic	Ambition
	Bridge
	Heaven
	Master
	Serena
	Vodka
The Prose Poem	Ignorance
	Marked
	Teacher
	Tumor

Spinning Jenny	Recluse
	Wedding
Tin House	Childhood
	Diagnosis
The Yale Literary Magazine	Amaryllis

"Marked" and "Tumor" were reprinted in *The Best of the Prose Poem: An International Journal,* Peter Johnson, ed. (White Pine Press, 2000).

A number of these poems appeared in a chapbook, *Think of It This Way* (Fameorshame Press, 2000), which was designed, illustrated, and printed by Paul Moxon.

My thanks to Aaron Anstett, Andrei Codrescu, Francine Conley, Nick Flynn, William Irwin, Jeff McDaniel, Rick Meier, Sarah Messer, Wendy Rawlings, Abraham Smith, Ellen Terrell, Steve Timm, Billy Vielvaso, James Wagner, and Kathy Whitcomb for their careful readings and vigorous criticism. Extraordinary thanks to Matt Freidson and Martha Rhodes for their extraordinary editorial guidance.

Finally, thanks to the Wisconsin Institute for Creative Writing and the National Endowment for the Arts. I began this series with the support of the former and completed it with the support of the latter.

Joel Brouwer's first book of poems, *Exactly What Happened* (Purdue University Press, 1999), won the Verna Emery Poetry Prize and the Larry Levis Reading Prize. He has received fellowships from the Mrs. Giles Whiting Foundation, the Bread Loaf Writer's Conference, the National Endowment for the Arts, and the Wisconsin Institute for Creative Writing. His poems and essays have appeared in *AGNI, Boston Review, Chelsea, Paris Review, Parnassus, Ploughshares, The Progressive, Southwest Review,* and other publications. He lives in Tuscaloosa, Alabama, and teaches at the University of Alabama.